National Theatre Connections
2015

PLAYS FOR YOUNG PEOPLE

Drama, Baby

Hood

The Boy Preference

The Edelweiss Pirates

Follow, Follow

The Accordion Shop

Hacktivists

Hospital Food

Remote

The Crazy Sexy Cool Girls' Fan Club

with an introduction by
ANTHONY BANKS

Bloomsbury Methuen Drama
An imprint of Bloomsbury Publishing Plc

B L O O M S B U R Y
LONDON · OXFORD · NEW YORK · NEW DELHI · SYDNEY

Bloomsbury Methuen Drama
An imprint of Bloomsbury Publishing Plc

50 Bedford Square   1385 Broadway
London   New York
WC1B 3DP   NY 10018
UK   USA

www.bloomsbury.com

BLOOMSBURY, METHUEN DRAMA and the Diana logo are trademarks of Bloomsbury Publishing Plc

First published 2015
Reprinted 2016

British Library Cataloguing-in-Publication Data
A catalogue record for this book is available from the British Library.

ISBN: PB: 978-1-4742-3768-0
ePub: 978-1-4742-3770-3
ePDF: 978-1-4742-3769-7

Library of Congress Cataloging-in-Publication Data
A catalog record for this book is available from the Library of Congress.

Typeset by Country Setting, Kingsdown, Kent CT14 8ES
Printed and bound in Great Britain

Contents

Introduction

Connections has been at the heart of the National Theatre's work for young people for the last two decades. The formula is simple: established playwrights create short plays for young actors to perform. Ten new plays are launched each year, building up a repertoire for young theatre companies to produce in schools, colleges and youth theatres. Each year more than 200 youth theatres and school groups from across the UK and beyond take up the challenge of staging a brand new play. Young people are involved not just as actors but as stage managers, designers, lighting and sound technicians – all roles required for a professional theatre production.

At the beginning of the rehearsal process, the NT hosts a weekend in the Clore Learning Centre and in our Studio in London for the directors of the youth theatre companies in the Connections programme. Here the directors get the chance to spend a day with the playwright, discussing the new play they're about to direct. When the plays are performed in the companies' home venues, a director from the National travels to see the performance, and provides detailed feedback in the form of a show report. All productions then transfer to a Connections festival held at professional theatres across the UK. One version of each play is invited to the final festival of the season which is held at the National Theatre.

The first collection of plays was published in 1995. The project was originally sponsored by British Telecom, who created the name 'Connections'. It has since enjoyed sponsorship from Accenture, Bank of America Merrill Lynch and Shell UK, and is now supported by a consortium of individual donors and from the NT's own core funds. Originally running bi-annually, Connections now runs every year, and since 1995 over 160 new plays have been commissioned, developed and performed by thousands of young actors across the country.

For more information and to get involved:
www.nationaltheatre.org.uk/connections

Connections 2015

Each year the National Theatre invites playwrights whose work excites us to write new plays for Connections. Playwrights take many different approaches to the commission but all Connections writers have the opportunity to test their ideas with young people through research, rehearsed readings and workshops. The ten plays in the 2015 collection were developed with young people across the UK.

JAMIE BRITTAIN first heard about Connections through his own youth theatre in Kendal, in the Lake District. Brewery Youth Theatre have been taking part in Connections since it began. As Jamie developed as a writer for television, creating among others the award-winning television series about teenage life *Skins*, he was following the plays in the Connections series. Subconsciously an idea was forming that led to his play DRAMA, BABY which is a touching, riotous, warm-hearted backstage comedy and a love letter to all those involved in studying and teaching drama in schools.

KATHERINE CHANDLER wrote a play about the struggles of parenthood in a working-class family called *Before It Rains* and won a Bruntwood award at the Royal Exchange in Manchester for her play *Bird*, about two girls in a care home, before she began to write her Connections play. HOOD takes the legend of Robin Hood and his Merry Men as its starting point, but is set on a contemporary housing estate and the main character Robyn is a girl. Katherine has created a world and a family of characters that she imagined she'd have liked to identify with when she was a girl. The play is about ambition, opportunity and determination, and the story is told in a way that is expressionistic at times, and full of potential for storytelling through physical theatre ensemble and puppetry.

ELINOR COOK wrote a play called *Microwave* which was developed at the National Theatre Studio and led to her winning the George Devine Award for Most Promising Playwright. She then wrote a play called *Girls' Guide to Saving the World* for the HighTide Festival in Suffolk. THE BOY PREFERENCE is a magical realist adventure set in the near future. It started when Elinor read about an Indian artist called Leena Kejwiral who created an art installation called *Missing* which illuminated the staggering effects of sex-selective abortion in certain countries in the world. This led Elinor to read many reports about girls who go missing, and inspired her to create a play with a central supernatural presence of young girls who return to the community that rejected them.

AYUB KHAN DIN has written several domestic comedies about Indian families living in the UK, *East Is East* and *Rafta Rafta* being two of the most widely performed and well loved. He took a different direction for Connections, writing an epic history play about Nazi youth in Cologne during the Second World War, loosely inspired by the structure and style of Brecht's play *Fear and Misery in the Third Reich*. The story of THE EDELWEISS PIRATES is based on the real-life gang of subversive students who were active in Cologne from 1938 until they were hanged in 1943. The central narrative of the play is laced with regular appearances from an ensemble providing a montage of historical context, and singers and dancers who surround the main action with snippets of music and dance from the time.

KATIE DOUGLAS wrote *Dig*, a highly acclaimed 45-minute play for new writing company Paines Plough about the impact of the economic downturn on ordinary lives, which was performed in several towns across the UK during 2011. Katie is part of the Royal Exchange Theatre Manchester's Bruntwood Hub group of writers, and has written extensively for television, including many episodes of *EastEnders* and *Waterloo Road* which is set in an urban comprehensive school. Originally from the west coast of Scotland but now living in London, Katie has returned to her home territory for the themes and story of her play about young people associated with an Orange Order march which is called FOLLOW, FOLLOW.

CUSH JUMBO worked as an actor at the National Theatre before becoming a playwright. She performed her first play *Josephine and I* herself at the Bush Theatre in West London. Her inspiration for writing THE ACCORDION SHOP was meeting an elderly shopkeeper called Mr Allodi, whose family ran an accordion shop on the high street near her home. Once Cush had written the various sections of the play, she workshopped it with some talented young actors at her old school, the Brit School in south London, who proved how flexible and suitable the script is for a large ensemble of young people.

BEN OCKRENT's early work includes the provocative short play *Honey*, about military strategists, which is part of the Tricycle Theatre's *The Great Game* cycle, a collection of plays about Afghanistan. Ben carried out a lot of research into the places known as 'hacker-spaces' before he started writing his Connections play HACKTIVISTS. He was fortunate to be given an introduction to the world of young hackers by the *Guardian* journalist Heather Brook, whose book *The Revolution Will Be Digitised* was a launch-pad in Ben's journey towards writing the play.

EUGENE O'HARE has worked frequently as an actor at the National Theatre, other London theatres and in his native Ireland. He has been writing for theatre and television for a few years and, through the Teenage Cancer Trust, was invited into a teenage cancer ward to spend a day talking to young patients to find the characters and stories for his Connections play, which is called HOSPITAL FOOD. Set in the adult-free zone of 'The Retreat', the various characters demonstrate how they're handling their illnesses both physically and psychologically. The play presents an extraordinarily vivid rush of human energy and spirit. Eugene was in a Connections play with the Newpoint Players Youth Company and his memories of that experience helped him to create the detailed young characters and their voices.

STEF SMITH emerged as a major voice when she wrote the text for the Olivier Award-winning play about sex trafficking *Roadkill*, which was originally produced at the Edinburgh Festival in 2010 and subsequently around Europe and the United States. Since then, Stef has won many other awards for her writing. Her Connections play REMOTE is about an act of protest and is set in real time over the course of an autumn evening in a park. Stef arrived at the idea after talking to young people in Aberdeen and Stirling about the 'remoteness' that can be experienced during years of adolescence, when the world can become a tricky place to engage with. Stef tested her script out with the wonderful PACE youth theatre in Paisley, Renfrewshire, before writing the final version of the play.

SARAH SOLEMANI wrote one of her first plays for the National Youth Theatre where she also started acting, and shortly after that wrote a play called *Up the Royal Borough* in response to Owen Jones's book *Chavs*. Sarah's Connections play is about a girls' fan club and a dysfunctional boy band. THE CRAZY SEXY COOL GIRLS' FAN CLUB runs a spiky commentary on the way the boy-band industry can send groups of young girls into a frenzy of obsession, tugging at their hearts and their purse strings. The comedy probes the temptation to join together as a group, and the instinct to strike out as an individual. The play itself behaves like a conjuring trick: from moment to moment in the story you're never entirely sure what is real and what is somebody's fantasy.

ANTHONY BANKS
National Theatre, March 2015